How Children Are Taught to Read

THE PROFESSIONAL EDUCATION SERIES

Walter K. Beggs, *Editor*
Dean Emeritus, Teachers College, and
Professor of Educational Administration
University of Nebraska

Royce H. Knapp, *Research Editor*
Regents Professor of Education
University of Nebraska

How Children Are Taught to Read

by

CAROLE MATTHES

Lincoln Public Schools
Lincoln, Nebraska

PROFESSIONAL EDUCATORS PUBLICATIONS, INC.
LINCOLN, NEBRASKA

Library of Congress Catalog Card No.: 72-77985

ISBN   0-88224-008-0

Contents

Introduction

"If I can read my name, how come I can't read any other words?" This exasperated, wondering statement of a five-year-old points out the excitement and thrill every child experiences in learning to read and wanting to read.

It is no wonder that parents, teachers and concerned adults keep searching for effective methods for teaching reading. Parents want the eagerness and desire to read to continue. Educators explore methods that over the long run will help the greatest number of readers make the greatest progress in reading.

Reading instruction has been a focal point of discussion for many years. More recently it is being discussed and critiqued by nonprofessionals on television, in periodicals, and in the press.

This current interest has promoted much controversy as to the "right way" to teach children to read.

At the outset, let us state there is no one miracle method that will teach all children to read. Children are individuals and will learn individually, using the approach or approaches most meaningful to them. Thus, the teacher must be familiar with all approaches and materials. Her professional skill enables her to diagnose what approach would be best suited for the needs and learning styles of a child.

Many questions are being asked concerning many of the different approaches being used in reading today. We will briefly review some of these current approaches to the teaching of reading in order possibly to answer some of these questions.

CHAPTER 1

The Basal Reading Approach

With little exception the basal reading approach has been the reading program in the United States. Surveys (1, p. 77) indicate that between 85 to 95 percent of all elementary schoolteachers use a basal reader as the core of their reading program.

No other area of the elementary school curriculum has been more discussed and researched than has reading, and the basal approach has predominantly been the facet most discussed. Some of the criticism hurled at this reading approach has been justified. To be sure, many teachers have accepted a basal reading program as a complete package, geared to all children. Thus, many children have not felt success in reading and have become discouraged and frustrated. The basal reading approach can be exciting and comprehensive in the hands of a flexible teacher, who has modified it to meet the needs of the children being taught.

A basal reading program is built around a coordinated series of materials that provide a sequential and systematic development of reading proficiency. This development can be characterized in one word — comprehensive. The approach is concerned with growth in all aspects of the reading act — word attack, comprehension, and critical analysis.

There are several major companies which publish basal reading series. Millions of dollars have been invested in the research and development of basal reading series. Basically they follow a similar pattern, yet have individual characteristics. The content of the material is, for the most part, a collection of adaptations of old or original selections. They are almost totally narrative in style.

The basal reading series usually comprises two to four paperback pre-primers. First-graders usually complete these as well as a primer and a first reader. There are two readers for grade two and two for grade three. In subsequent grades (some series extend through grade nine) there is only one reader for each grade. Accompanying each reader is a teacher's guide or manual, explaining the philosophy of the program, telling in detail how to teach each selection, and suggesting skill activities and other related ideas. Besides the regular reader, every pupil also has a workbook containing exercises designed to help him learn various reading skills.

Most publishers supplement their reading materials with diagnostic tests, supplementary readers for either independent or guided reading, records and filmstrips, overhead transparencies, ditto masters of skill worksheets, and games and devices.

A basal reading approach focuses on three objectives in guiding the development of the program—scope, sequence, and organization.

SCOPE

In a basal reading approach, the scope of the program refers to the range of skills and content theme. The organization of systematically presented word study and comprehension skills is one of the strong points of the basal approach. For the beginning reader particularly, the reader is very dependent in this part of the program. The teacher's guide provides the teacher with instructional plans and exercises for skill development. The stories in the basal reader provide practice in the use of the skills being taught as materials are used. Teachers are encouraged to use diagnostic teaching procedures and then select activities appropriate for the children they are teaching. In grouping and adjusting instruction, basic reading series can be used to provide differentiated instruction.

SEQUENCE

Sequence refers to the order given to the teaching of various elements with which the program is concerned. Each developmental step grows out of those preceding and at the same time serves as a foundation for the ones following. Thus, essential sequential development is organized into learning experiences by the basal program. Reading is a very complex learning task; therefore, sequential development is most necessary.

Developmental psychologists have had a profound influence upon the construction of basal reading skills. The theory that children pass through developmental "states" was adapted to the design of reading programs. A developmental reading stage is an arbitrarily defined period of time during which certain skills, attitudes, and interests are developed. Within the basal reader the emphasis on sequential development is evident in the levels of pupil interest, pupil understanding, and difficulty of the material.

The difficulty level is shown when sequentially the sentences become longer and more involved. The number of new words is increased and the selections become longer. More complicated plots and character development are also evident. As the child develops competencies in the fundamental reading skills, he progresses into material designed to stress comprehension skills. Being able to make deductions, generalize, and exercise critical thinking are in the later stages of development.

ORGANIZATION

The organization of the basal series is designed to bring a total working and integrated relationship to the children, through the skills, the teaching methods, and instructional materials. This is done in the development and use of the total program.

ROLE OF THE TEACHER

As with any reading approach, the key to its effective use is with the teacher. The basal reading approach provides such excellent materials that it is very easy for a teacher to follow closely each page of the guide day after day, month after month. However, adaptations must be made to fit the backgrounds, skill development, and learning rates of the children involved. Thus, the teacher uses the basal approach as a foundation on which to build other reading experiences. The teacher must be able to provide additional reading materials on Alaskan Eskimos after the children have read a basal story on living in an igloo. Trade books, magazines, pictures are provided to meet interests and reading levels of the children involved.

Teaching a basal reading lesson involves the following steps:

I.   Introduction
     A. Motivate the story to be read
     B. Introduce the new vocabulary
II. Directed Reading
     A. Ask oral questions
     B. Read silently to find answers
     C. Oral discussion after each section read
III. Oral Reading
     A. Purposeful — in response to questions
     B. Guiding Interpretation
IV. Skill Development
     A. Word attack skills
     B. Interpretation skills
     C. Vocabulary development
     D. Practice of these skills (workbook)
V.   Supplementary Activities
     A. Enrichment activities
     B. Special activities

This basic outline is commonly employed with each basal reader selection. The material should be taught in order of its presentation because the vocabulary and skills are presented in sequential arrangement. Usually two or more reading periods will be needed to complete a selection. This, of course, depends on the level, the children's abilities, and the length of the material.

ADVANTAGES OF THE BASAL APPROACH

1. The basal reading series is a comprehensive reading program providing systematic instruction from pre-readiness through upper elementary grades.

2. The teachers' guides provide suggestions and a step-by-step outline for teaching. This is most helpful for the beginning teacher.

3. The reading skills of word recognition and comprehension are presented in a systematic step-by-step order.

4. The materials are carefully scaled in difficulty and arranged in a sequential pattern.

5. The selections are well rounded reading choices, illustrated by selected artists.

6. The same characters are often used, especially in beginning readers. This gives the child a feeling of familiarity with the material and adds to his confidence in reading.

7. Often the content of the material deals with experiences and interests common to the child reading the selection.

8. A basic or core vocabulary is established, using much repetition in the material. This is a built-in factor which should prevent frustration on the part of the reader.

9. This approach provides diagnostic tools to discover pupil strengths and weaknesses.

10. Preparation of the materials is usually the work of several reading experts, thus making a more conclusive program than one teacher could prepare.

11. A basal series may permit the teacher much flexibility in dealing with individual differences because of the materials provided and the extra activities suggested.

DISADVANTAGES OF THE BASAL APPROACH

1. The approach may contribute to a stereotyped, uncreative type of teaching.

2. Often the approach strictly limits the reading done by the child to that of just the basal reader.

3. Basal readers and their manuals encourage group instruction rather than concentrating on individual differences and needs.

4. The manual contains much material to help the teacher. Who guides the inexperienced teacher to distinguish between essentials and nonessentials?

5. For many years basal readers have been geared for middle-class, white suburban children, excluding any other races or lifestyles.

6. The financial investment in a series is expensive.

7. Basal readers often fail to provide an adequate foundation for reading in other content areas.

8. The basal approach is overly dependent upon the visual or sight word method. This, however, does depend upon the company publishing the material.

9. This approach may monopolize classroom time and leave little or no time for creative activities.

10. Very often the material is too difficult for the lower third of the class, and at the same time be insufficiently challenging for the superior children.

11. Skills may be developed in isolation from the reading act, yet transfer is assumed.

RESEARCH

There is probably no other approach that has been researched as much as the basal reading program. Each series has some unique qualities.

The United States Office of Education sponsored a study (1, pp. 488-90) which involved close to a thousand first- and second-grade children. Their growth in a basal reading program compared to other programs was studied. Some of their findings showed:

1. A basal reading program with supplementary phonics materials (in addition to those commonly supplied with the basal) produces significantly greater achievement in reading than basal materials alone.

2. Children in the basal program read significantly more books than those in the contrasting programs, while children in a basal plus phonics system showed the most positive attitudes toward reading.

In the second year of the study it was found:

1. Among low-ability pupils, the basal pupils averaged one-third of a grade level higher than any other programs in comprehension.

2. Children in the basal program continue to show much wider reading experience than in other programs. This particular study, comparing a basal, a basal plus phonics, the Lippencott system,

and ITA showed no consistent trend toward superiority of any of these studied.

SUMMARY

The basal reading approach is the most widely used in the United States. Authors and publishers are continually changing their series to respond to the continuous barrage of criticism. Thus, the basal reader will probably continue to be the most popular reading approach for some time.

What does that mean to the teacher now taking training, or the parent concerned about his child's reading progress? It means, the reading teacher will find an organized, sequential basal program outlined to be taught—but the key to success in teaching the child will still be in the individual teacher's art and proficiency. He can use or misuse the basal approach. Too often teachers have considered the basal manual or teacher's guide the absolute with no digression provided. A good teacher uses the guide as a guide supplementing, enriching, and creating other experiences as the child's needs so warrant.

The basal reading series is one of the most carefully designed, elaborately constructed tools a teacher has at his disposal. It should be used as just that—a tool—one of several to help meet the needs of children.

REFERENCES

1. Spache, George D., and Evelyn B. Spache. *Reading in the Elementary School*. Boston: Allyn and Bacon, Inc., 1969.

SUPPLEMENTARY REFERENCES

1. Anderson, Verna Dieckman. *Reading and Young Children*. New York: The Macmillan Company, 1968.
2. Chall, Jeanne. *Learning to Read: The Great Debate*. New York: McGraw-Hill, 1967. Chapter 3.

3. Durkin, Dolores. *Teaching Them to Read*. Boston, New York: Allyn and Bacon, Inc., 1970. Pp. 103-45.

4. Gans, Roma. *Common Sense in Teaching Reading*. Chicago, Illinois: Bobbs-Merrill Co., 1963. Pp. 300-32.

5. Habecker, James E. *"How Can We Improve Basic Readers?" Elementary English*, XXXVI (December, 1959). Pp. 560-63.

6. Strang, Ruth. *Helping Your Child Improve His Reading*. New York: E. P. Dutton and Co., 1962. Chapter 5.

CHAPTER 2

Language-Experience Approach

The language-experience approach to the teaching of reading recognizes that learning to read is dependent on a child's oral language background. It recognizes the close relationship among reading, speaking, writing, and listening. The child's experiences in the language areas before entering school and during his school years will be a determining factor as to how well he will progress in his reading. Children cannot cope with ideas or language in a reading program which is advanced beyond their own listening or speaking vocabulary.

DEFINITION

Recognizing this close relationship between the four facets of language, equality of emphasis is placed on all the communication skills. The language-experience approach weaves speaking, listening, reading, and writing into the complete fabric of a child's development.

The method used in teaching by the language-experience approach is stated in the words of a child (2, pp. 33-35):

What I can think about, I can talk about
What I can say I can write (or someone can write for me)
What I can write, I can read.

In defining the skills developed in the language-experience approach to reading Allen (2) lists 20:

1. Sharing experiences — The ability to tell or illustrate something on a purely personal basis.

2. Discussion experiences—The ability to interact with what other people say and write.

3. Listening to stories—The ability to hear what others have to say and relate it to their own experiences.

4. Telling stories—The ability to organize one's thinking so that it can be shared orally or through dictation in a clear and interesting manner.

5. Dictating—The ability to choose, from all that might be said, the most important part for someone else to write and read.

6. Developing speaking, writing, and reading relationships—The ability to conceptualize reading as speech that has been written.

7. Making and reading books—The ability to organize one's ideas into a form that others can use and the ability to use the ideas which others have shared through books.

8. Developing an awareness of common vocabulary—The ability to recognize that our language contains many common words and patterns of expression.

9. Expanding vocabulary—The ability to expand one's vocabulary through listening and speaking, followed by writing and reading.

10. Writing independently—The ability to write one's own ideas and present them in a form for others to read.

11. Reading whole books—The ability to read books for information, recreation, and improvement of reading skills on an individualized and personalized basis.

12. Improving style and form—The ability to profit from listening to and reading well written materials.

13. Using a variety of resources—The ability to recognize and use many resources in expanding vocabulary, improving oral and written expression, and sharing.

14. Reading a variety of symbols—The ability to read symbols —the clock, calendar, radio dial, and thermometer—in their total environment.

15. Studying words—The ability to find the correct pronunciation and meaning of words and to spell the words in writing activities.

16. Improving comprehension—The ability, through oral and written activities, to gain skill in following directions, understanding

words in the context of sentences and paragraphs, reproducing the thought in a passage, and reading for general significance.

17. Outlining—The ability to use various methods of briefly restating ideas in the order in which they were written or spoken.

18. Summarizing—The ability to get the main impression, outstanding ideas, or details of what has been read or spoken.

19. Integrating and assimilating ideas—The ability to use reading and listening for specific purposes of a personal nature.

20. Reading critically—The ability to determine the validity and reliability of statements.

The reading program is not like any other approach mentioned in this publication. Not based on a particular series of reading materials or on individualized reading library, this approach takes its foundation in the oral and written expression of the children. The child learns to read his own thoughts as they are written down. How meaningful an experience for a child eager to learn—his own story! This motivation continues as he writes, reads, and dictates his thoughts on experiences meaningful to him. The child's progress depends on the experiences and the expansion into oral language and his own written expression.

THE TEACHER'S ROLE

In implementing this program, the teacher encourages the child to share his ideas and experiences through his oral expression as he creates pictures, paints, or works with clay. Then he explains the picture to the teacher and the other children. The teacher writes down the dictated story. In time the child can write stories with less and less help from the teacher. He can then read stories to the class and can eventually read the stories other children have written.

The teacher leads the group of children in writing an experience chart. A field trip, a new pet, a recipe, any shared experience becomes the focal point as the teacher summarizes the children's ideas and discoveries as they dictate them. The charts then become a group reading experience. During the writing of the chart, word choice, sentence structure, and the sounds of letters and words are discussed. When the child begins to break through to written expression, the beginning of his actual instruction in reading and writing is appropriate.

Devices such as lists of words to be recognized on sight, picture dictionaries, labels on classroom objects, and other children's charts help pupils to rapidly extend their writing and reading vocabularies.

After several weeks of experience with group-composed charts, small groups can be formed within the class. By this grouping, there is more opportunity for stimulating group or individual stories.

During the first grade, labeling paintings, reading and completing sentences (I like to_____.), classroom newspapers, and the writing of groups of rhyming words, lead rapidly toward an introduction to individualized, free reading and increased development of self-expression.

By the second grade, children might be producing their own charts, composing stories, or book reports. The third grade emphasizes the writing of poetry or song lyrics, still based on a variety of group experiences. Always available are various simple readers, trade books, and science books, used as resource materials for ideas, for vocabulary, enrichment, spelling, and other purposes. As far as phonics instruction is concerned, the child learns to represent letters by the sounds he wishes to record on paper on a "say it"-"see it" basis. Emphasis is purely on translating sounds of oral language into written form; there are no predetermined sequences of training in word recognition skills or any other major reading skills. Evaluation, also, is based on pupil form, and ability to comprehend and interpret the writings of others.

Because the language-experience approach makes it possible for the child to identify from the beginning with reading material, and likewise, be motivated to read material because it is his experience, and therefore, something he can understand, the method is an effective one for a teacher to use, especially with the culturally different child. Such a child frequently has a different speech pattern which causes him to distort words, which in turn leads to a meager recognition and understanding of them. Too often, the culturally different child will meet words in print which are not of his understanding or speaking vocabulary. When the child is able to write and read his own material, he will naturally have a feeling of accomplishment to add to his self-esteem. Also, this approach provides an excellent opportunity for children to learn how to take notes, to outline, to organize, and to read critically. While the approach is versatile and informal, it must be carefully and thoughtfully planned. It must be preceded by a carefully prepared adequate readiness program, and provisions must be made for teaching word attack or various comprehension skills. Although the language experience approach is more often thought of as a reading approach for primary grades, actually, there is no reason why it could not be just as effective in the intermediate grades.

RESEARCH: SAN DIEGO COUNTY
READING RESEARCH (1)

This approach was first tested along with other approaches in the Reading Study Project of San Diego County. During the 1959-60 school year, these schools undertook a major program of improving reading instruction. The study was built around an exploration of three approaches to the teaching of reading—the basal, the individualized, and the language experience. The study describes the approaches used. No definite conclusions are drawn as to the benefits of one approach above others.

ADVANTAGES OF THE LANGUAGE-
EXPERIENCE APPROACH

1. The language-experience approach integrates the various facets of speaking, writing, reading, and listening instruction in the curriculum.

2. The importance of each child's own oral-language background is recognized and utilized in printed form.

3. It helps children become increasingly sensitive to their environment by discussing and recording their experiences.

4. Language development is assured in a program that encourages self-expression in many media throughout the day.

5. This type of approach promotes confidence in language usage. It creates a desire to rework and refine one's own language.

6. The development of language experiences gives depth of meaning to art and construction activities. Discussion, verbal and written, is used as a reading lesson for many activities.

7. It shows children that reading is talk written down. It makes reading a meaningful experience to each child.

8. It encourages greater creative experience in writing original stories.

9. It provides a source of materials for the culturally deprived child.

10. Children learn to share their own ideas — but, more importantly, they learn to listen to the ideas of others.

DISADVANTAGES OF THE LANGUAGE-EXPERIENCE APPROACH

1. A child's reading experiences and development will be extremely limited if he only experiences his own written expressions.

2. There is no planned sequence of reading skills but purely incidental or accidental learning of these skills.

3. There is no concrete method to evaluate or record the child's progress.

4. Children may have difficulty in the transition of reading and comprehending the written expression of other children or other books.

5. This approach falsely assumes that the reading, writing, speaking, and listening vocabularies of children are equally developed and can be easily transferred from one vocabulary to another. But, research proves this false because of the fact that speaking and listening vocabularies are far greater developed than reading and writing vocabularies.

6. The children would have no real means of attacking a word that was unfamiliar to them — or to their listening language. Having no way of decoding a new word, this could result in a child having problems in reading.

SUMMARY

The language-experience method has been widely accepted, as it does not limit teachers or pupils to books of particular grade levels. Books become a resource tool rather than a basic device to teach children to read. Books and readers help supply the vicarious experiences, the depth of meanings for the words which the child needs to express his ideas in oral and written work. Many other classroom and extra-classroom activities, plus teacher instruction and demonstration, further this development in thinking and in expression of language.

In this approach to reading, the level of language at which the beginner functions is not highly significant. He may be language-deprived, or facile in the use of words. His progress becomes an individual matter; each child gradually develops a broader and deeper skill with words and moves toward more complex language patterns which help him to convey his thoughts.

REFERENCES

1. Department of Education, San Diego County. *Report of the Reading Study Project,* Monograph No. 1 of the Reading Study Project. San Diego: Superintendent of Schools, 1961.
2. Lee, Dorris M., and R. V. Allen. *Learning to Read Through Experience,* Second Edition. New York: Appleton-Century-Crofts, Meredith Corporation, 1963.

SUPPLEMENTARY READING

1. Allen, R. V., and Allen, Claryce. *Language Experience in Reading.* Chicago: Encyclopaedia Britannica Press, 1966.
2. Allen, R. V. "How a Language Experience Program Works," *A Decade of Innovations.* Newark, Del.: International Reading Association, 1968. Pp. 1-29.
3. Batinick, Mary Ellen. "Language Experience Activities," *The Reading Teacher.* Newark: I.R.A., March, 1970. Pp. 539-46.
4. Crutchfield, M. A. "In Practice: The Language Experience Approach to Reading," *Elementary English,* XV, March, 1960, Pp. 285-88.
5. Hildreth, Gertrude. "Early Writing as an Aid to Reading," *Elementary English,* 40 (January, 1963). Pp. 15-20.

6. Stauffer, Russell G. "The Language-Experience Approach," *First Grade Reading Programs*, James F. Kerfoot, ed. Perspectives in Reading, No. 5. Newark, Del.: International Reading Association, 1965.

CHAPTER 3

The Individualized Approach

For the past few years we have heard more and more discussion on the importance of individualizing instruction. Educators have agreed that children must develop at their own pace rather than be limited to group grade-leveled expectations. The problem has been how to implement such a program within the classroom.

DEFINITION

Discussion currently centers upon this implementation. The term "individualization" has many definitions. To one person it means a one-to-one tutoring situation. Others interpret it as a larger teacher-pupil ratio. For the purposes of this discussion, we will consider the individualized reading approach as not one concerned with the number of children being taught but with the appropriateness of what is taught for each child.

Within this framework, there are still many different plans. Jeannette Veatch (3) and Walter Barbe (1) have outlined specific individualized reading programs. Guidelines, checklists, schedules, and charts are presented in outlining the aspects of their programs. In contrast to a specific program, many educators define individualized reading within the framework of an organizational plan which would involve staff utilization to implement the program. Involvement of paraprofessionals, team teaching, and elaborate record-keeping for some people are synonomous with individualized instruction. For the purposes of this discussion we will center our thoughts on the individualized reading program rather than the organizational plan, which will be discussed later.

Individualized reading as reported in many programs and research has three main aspects: self-selection, conferences, and diagnosis.

SELF-SELECTION

A child selects his own reading material, suited to his interests and reading ability. He reads this chosen material by himself and at his own pace. One of the "musts" in this approach is the necessity of a large number and variety of trade and textbooks. Books should be available on every conceivable subject and on a wide range of reading levels. Their appeal should be such that the children want to read them. This built-in motivational factor capturing a child's interests and his reading ability determines his choice. Teachers cannot assume that they can meet all the needs and interests for all pupils. This self-selection, however, helps to meet these needs, giving the child a sense of importance and worth.

A classroom library should contain an ample supply of trade (library) books, basal readers of several series and grade levels, books of high interest and low level of difficulty, books the children have made, children's newspapers and magazines, reading games, self-directional instructional reading materials. Books and materials should be available on every conceivable subject interesting to a child and at different levels of reading difficulty. Some schools are using five copies of six different supplementary reading books which cost little, if any more, than thirty copies of the same book. Inexpensive paper-bound books from bookstores, bookmobiles, the public library, or carefully screened books from home are all places where books can be obtained.

Children read their choice at their own pace. Under this program, the gifted child progresses at his own pace; the slow reader is not publicly stigmatized. Each child can display success for all to see. During this period there is usually some time set aside for written activities. These can be either creative pursuits in writing or the arts or the skill-oriented activities. In either case the activities are closely aligned with the reading the children are currently pursuing. Unhampered by pressure to finish quickly or wait for slow readers, a child finds the real pleasure and satisfaction of reading for his own enjoyment. The teacher is aware of his individual pace during conferences.

CONFERENCES

Conference time is when the child shares with his teacher his feelings about his current reading choice. This close personal relationship serves the child's psychological needs. The teacher focuses her whole attention on the child and assures the child of an appreciative audience. The child will not have to share this time with any other class members: this is completely his own time with his teacher. These conferences may be administered either at the teacher's desk, or as the teacher circulates around the room, responding to requests for help.

During the conference time, discussion is centered on the current reading choice, progress in any research activities, check comprehension in silent reading and listen to his oral reading, although the latter is not an essential part.

Some authorities recommend between two and four conferences a week. This probably is dependent on the degree of self-direction the child has achieved and his reading proficiency. Some children may need a conference daily, others only once a week. The teacher's diagnosis is the determining factor as to the number of conferences.

The teacher must be skillful in questioning and listening, making the conference stimulating, enjoyable, and instructional.

Questions the teacher may use are:

1. How does the child feel about the reading in general and about his selected pieces?

2. What skills need reteaching or regrouping? Should the child be assigned to a group for instruction or should he be assigned independent work?

3. Does he read well orally?

On the basis of this conference, an individual diagnosis and prescription is made.

DIAGNOSIS

Diagnosis is the teacher's main role in an individualized reading program. The teacher must have goals outlined and skills identified before beginning a program. Within the framework of this plan, she must know how to teach the skills and how to utilize the most appropriate material for developing the skills. The teacher must also use available general and objective tests to test specific skills within the broad reading areas.

Individualized reading emphasizes the rewards of reading, but the teacher must have a system of evaluating, checking, and recording the progress of each pupil. Specific details are noted so that it is known what level of reading achievement each child has gained.

In an individualized approach, children are not taught skills unless they need them. Skills may be taught to a single child, to a group, or to a whole class. Children are placed in short-term groups on the basis of their skill needs. Once the skill is mastered and application assured, that particular group is discontinued. Children are grouped for other objectives, too. Discussion, like interests, research and projects stemming from their personal reading become the factors for group membership. Many of these groups share their experiences with the rest of the class, thus sharing their reading choices with others and promoting more interest. Oral reading is promoted by a genuine audience situation which serves to promote the art of speaking and listening. The children want to read, and reading becomes its own reward.

The success of the whole program depends on how materials are used for diagnosis and how the program is developed. Thus, its success also rests upon the teacher's proficiency.

THE TEACHER'S ROLE

Individualized instruction in reading emphasizes the role of the teacher as a diagnostician and prescriber. The success or failure of a given program is completely up to the teacher. This type of program is not for the poorly organized teacher, a poor disciplinarian, or an unambitious teacher. The teacher must be resourceful, flexible, and constantly aware of the needs of the children.

Competence in teaching reading skills is a necessity. Thus, this program is usually not for the beginning teacher. The matching of appropriate materials with needed skills for a particular child takes real professional competence. The success of the whole program depends on how materials are used for diagnosis and how it is developed. Teachers go from large to small groups, to individuals, back to group work, meeting differences in the classroom.

Individualized reading focuses on the child as a reader more than the teacher as a teacher. The child truly involved in this program finds real self-fulfillment. This type of program should promote one of the greatest rewards of teaching — seeing a love for learning develop in children. Thus, a teacher needs individualized teaching as greatly as children need an individualized program.

ADVANTAGES OF THE INDIVIDUALIZED READING PROGRAM

1. Practical experience shows that children do exercise a remarkable ability to select appropriate books when: (a) there is sufficient varied reading matter available; (b) the teacher guides but does not compel choices; and (c) children are free to discontinue reading a book when they find that it does not come up to their expectations in one way or another. Self-selected books are more likely to satisfy reading interests. The child's interest is not that of the group, nor teacher-motivated, it is personal interest. This interest is paramount and is captured before the child is taught. This self-selection helps promote extensive independent reading.

2. There is greater opportunity for interaction among pupils in bringing together ideas gained from their independent reading. This impact on self-selection of the process of "sharing" should not be overlooked. Word-of-mouth information about books among the boys and girls is another potent force in determining which books will be selected. Oral reading is promoted only by a genuine audience situation which serves to promote the art of speaking and listening.

3. The child progresses at his own rate, depending on his ability. This individualized development builds self-confidence

and self-motivation in the children. Each child experiences greater self-worth and takes more initiative.

4. The individual teacher-pupil conferences help establish a close personal relationship. This one-to-one teacher-pupil conference helps develop very favorable reading attitudes. This conference also encourages teachers to observe, diagnose reading weaknesses, and provide guidance to help children overcome their difficulties.

5. Recitation during group instruction is frequently wasteful, since each child actually participates for only a fractional part of the class period. Individualized instruction gives each child an opportunity to work independently and to function effectively every moment of the instructional period.

6. Individualized reading removes the distinction between "slow" and "fast" readers. The program diminishes the competition and comparison, avoiding the stigma of being in the lowest group. Unfavorable comparison with the other children is lessened.

7. The program is very flexible, adaptable to any group. This makes the success dependent on the proficiency of the teacher and her ability to organize and plan. No ceiling on the learning makes it even more adaptable to top readers who are especially responsive.

8. Individualized reading rejects the lockstep instruction which tended to become standardized within the framework of the graded system and traditional graded materials.

DISADVANTAGES OF THE INDIVIDUALIZED READING PROGRAM

1. One of the main arguments against an individualized reading program is that there is a strong danger of insufficient skill development. In the short conference period, can the teacher accurately diagnose the weakness a child may have in attacking a new word or developing comprehension skills? This lack of systematic development of reading is a real problem to children who need definite sequentially taught tools to unlock new words.

2. Once some skill groups are identified there is some question as to the permanence of the skills taught when the period is so brief. Thus, it is important that teachers know all sequences of reading

skills and provide systematic instruction in these developmental skills.

3. Teachers must be proficient in the conferencing techniques —questioning, listening, and diagnosing. Many teachers do not have the necessary skills to diagnose and remedy individual children's weaknesses. This short period of conference time must be used to maximum amount of gain.

4. Keeping records in an individualized reading program is a mammoth job. In order to know each child's strengths and weaknesses a teacher must have records of his reading. The organization and effectiveness of this clerical burden is again as good as the teacher.

5. It becomes difficult to provide enough books to meet each child's interests and level of ability. Inadequate library materials present a problem in implementing this program.

6. Young children need much guidance in material selection. For this reason many individualized reading programs begin with post-primer readers.

7. Reading quantities of books in a single area of interest or at the same reading level will not develop reading maturity.

8. Slow pupils and others who cannot work well independently become restless and tend to waste time. The self-directional ability is present at different levels within group members. It is important to identify the slower moving individuals and conference more frequently with them.

9. Individualized reading makes little or no provision for readiness.

10. No effort is made in advance to deal with unknown words, specific word meanings which are peculiar to the context, or difficult concepts.

11. In individualized reading the guidance follows the completion of reading, thereby making no provision for the avoidance of errors and a reduction in reinforcement of inappropriate responses.

12. Individualized reading presupposes the availability of a great number of titles from which the child may choose. This is not being idealistic. It also presupposes that the teacher is thoroughly familiar with the contents of these books. Are teachers so acquainted with hundreds of books that they may be able in

discussing them with the children to probe beneath the mere surface?

RESEARCH

Does individualized reading really work? Here are some reports on experimental studies on the merits of individualized reading when compared to the basal reading program:

> Commenting on an unpublished doctoral study made by Clare Walker (New York University) in grades four, five, and six Robert Karlin observed: One experiment has been completed in Michigan. Two groups of children were matched and taught by student teachers under the supervision of critic teachers. One group followed a basal reader approach, while the other engaged in individualized reading. The data showed no significant differences between the groups in reading gains. The student teachers did report that the children in the individualized group showed greater interest in reading and read more books than the children in the basal reader group. (4, pp. 125-26)

In January, 1961, Irene Vite reported on experimental studies on the subject of individualized reading instruction versus basal instruction. Of seven studies, four showed significant test results favoring individualized reading while three showed results favoring basal reading. One researcher who found negative test-score results for individualized reading still concluded that in other factors—more books read by the children, better study habits, better attitude toward reading—the findings favored individualized reading. (4, pp. 126-27)

The following conclusion was drawn from studies taken in Los Angeles County. Seventy-two classroom teachers and 2,485 pupils from kindergarten through sixth grade were involved in a three-year study with individualized reading techniques.

> It may tentatively be suggested that: (a) For the majority of the individual pupils in the seven classes the use of individualized

reading techniques resulted in lower gains in reading achievement over a period of one calendar year, when contrasted with
the results of other methods of reading instruction that are currently being used in this district and throughout the nation;
(b) the use of self-selective reading methods achieved no significantly different results with the superior students than with
average students; and (c) the use of individualized reading
techniques resulted in no significant difference in growth between reading vocabulary and reading comprehension. (2, pp.
216-17)

SUMMARY

Individualized reading is another attempt to adjust to the wide
range of reading capabilities in any one class and to the differing
rates at which children achieve in this complex learning. A large
amount of reading material at many levels, and on many subjects,
in the classroom collection of books is an essential feature of an
individualized approach to reading. To satisfy the classroom de-
mands for quantity and variety of reading matter, an excellent
school library is essential. Each child selects his reading material,
paces himself, and keeps records of his progress. Under this
method, used even in grade one, each pupil reads widely, materials
of his own choice. The child is allowed to set his own pace even if
it means he reads relatively little over a period of time. Once or
twice a week, the teacher meets with the child in a pupil-teacher
conference for five or ten minutes. The teacher uses the conference
time to find out what the child has read since the last conference, to
evaluate by means of carefully thought-out questions the degree of
comprehension, to take note of special needs and difficulties and
give specific help with these, and to keep a careful record of the
child's reading capabilities and needs and his developmental progress. The teacher guides the child, to some extent, in future choice
of material. Occasionally, the teacher groups the children who have
the same reading need into a temporary special group to teach them
the required reading skill or to provide classroom remediation.
Also, there are often small-groups or whole-class sharing periods,
during which one or more children share with the other children
material selected for that purpose.

Individualized reading programs can work, but they may not always be successful. Not every approach to teaching reading can be successfully applied to all children; and any method is always dependent upon the quality of the teaching. Individualized reading, can, however, be a very exciting, worthwhile experience for students and teacher.

REFERENCES

1. Barbe, Walter. *Educator's Guide to Personalized Reading Instruction.* Englewood Cliffs, New Jersey: Prentice-Hall, Inc. 1961.
2. Durr, William K. *Reading Instruction.* Boston, New York: Houghton-Mifflin Company, 1967.
3. Veatch, Jeannette. *Individualizing Your Reading Program.* New York: G. P. Putnam's Sons, 1959.
4. West, Roland. *Individualizing Reading Instruction.* New York: Kennikat Press, 1965.

SUPPLEMENTARY READING

1. Barbe, Walter B. *Teaching Reading: Selected Materials.* New York: Oxford Press, 1965.
2. Dechant, Emerald V. *Improving the Teaching of Reading.* New Jersey: Prentice-Hall, Inc., 1964. Pp. 208-13.
3. Dolch, E. W. "Individualized Reading vs. Group Reading," *Elementary English,* XXVIII (December, 1961), pp. 566-75, and XXXIX (January, 1962) pp. 14-21.
4. Esbensen, Thorwald. *Working with Individualized Instruction: The Duluth Experience.* Belmont, California: Fearon Publishers, 1968.
5. Howes, Virgil M. *Individualizing Instruction in Reading and Social Studies.* New York: Macmillan Company, 1970.
6. Mazurkiewics, Albert. *New Perspectives in Reading Instruction.* New York: Pitman Publishing Corporation, 1964.
7. Schubert, Delwyn G. *Improving Reading Through Individualized Correction.* Dubuque, Iowa: Wm. C. Brown Publishers, 1968.

8. Spache, George D., and Evelyn B. Spache. *Reading in the Elementary School*. Boston: Allyn and Bacon, 1969.

CHAPTER 4

The Linguistic Approach

For most classroom teachers linguistics and the linguistic approach to reading instruction is viewed with uncertainty, based mainly on lack of understanding. Much of this lack of understanding is due to the fact that linguistics is in itself a scholarly science requiring years of study and investigation. Absence of widely accepted classroom materials in the teaching of reading using this linguistic approach is another reason that promotes uncertainty.

DEFINITION

Before exploring the main facets of this reading approach, it would be wise to acquaint ourselves with some of the terminology used in this science as it applies to reading instruction:

Linguistics (4)	"We can define linguistics as an old and scholarly field which scientifically observes language in action as a means for determining how the language developed, how it functions today and how it is currently evolving."
Phoneme /b/	A phoneme is an individual speech sound. Most linguists agree there are about 44 phonemes in the English language.
Grapheme b	A grapheme is a letter or group of letters that represent a phoneme.
Morpheme boy boys boyish	A morpheme is a word and its meaningful parts. It is concerned with the use of roots, prefixes, suffixes, and inflectional endings as they influence meaning.

Syntax   Syntax is the way in which words are put to-
The boy caught gether in a meaningful order.
  the ball.

The linguist views written language as a second code. It is a
graphic representation of the phonemes or speech sounds. The first
code being that of the phonemes. With a few exceptions, which we
shall discuss, linguistics has not given us a system of reading instruction, but some valid information about the nature, structural
properties, and operations of language. This is because a linguist's
primary concern is that of oral communication. There cannot be a
linguistic approach to reading instruction because the science of
linguistics is not concerned with teaching children to read. Never-
theless, many linguists have become interested in the teaching of
reading and how their science might enlighten the area.

One such linguist was Leonard Bloomfield. Bloomfield wrote
an article in 1942 (1) that outlined his ideas on the teaching of
reading. He was very critical of phonic methods, particularly those
using a blending procedure. His criticism was also aimed at the
word method, which he compared to the study of Chinese
ideographs.

Briefly, his recommended procedure included the following
ideas (5):

1. Start with teaching the identification of all alphabet letters
by name (not by sound).

2. Begin with words in which each letter represents only one
phonetic value, avoiding words with silent letters or less common
sounds, so that beginning words consist of three-letter words with
a consonant-vowel-consonant pattern containing only short vowels.

3. Use the principle of minimal variation, employing a list of
words alike except for one letter, such as ban, Dan, can, fan, man,
and the like.

4. Do not teach rules about letter-sound correspondences, the
children will evolve correct responses when sound and spelling
correspond in regular fashion.

5. Employ the learned words in sentences, such as "Nan, can,
fan, Dan."

Developing and expanding Bloomfield's theories was Clarence Barnhart, who in 1961 wrote a book (2) on a linguistic approach to reading.

Since this time several companies have published reading series that are based on linguistic principles. They have some similarities in that "decoding" or changing a printed code into verbal communication is the primary consideration. Most of the materials advocate a whole-word approach, rather than any sounding or blending procedures. Some materials do not include illustrations, saying they are distracting to the reader.

THE TEACHER'S ROLE

This newest approach in reading has brought into the forefront a greater awareness of language on the part of the classroom teacher and its role in child development. Linguists have awakened interest and study in this area and more is being done to add to our knowledge of language acquisition. Teachers of reading can learn much from linguists about the science of language.

The classroom teacher applies some of the basic linguistic principles by:

1. Providing experiences so that the children are aware that reading is really familiar talk written down.

2. Before a child reads, his own speech should reflect the vocabulary, language structures, and intonations which he will meet in the reading material.

3. The reading matter used in beginning reading should not be used until the child has shown fluency in his own talking and listening of the words he will be reading.

One of the major teaching methods employed in this approach is that of teaching spelling patterns. Words are selected based on similar spelling patterns. The child is encouraged to arrive at the difference a letter makes in a word as cat-fat, cat-mat, mat-fat, etc.

The linguistic readers focus on words rather than isolated sounds. Linguistic readers actually use what could be called a whole-word approach in which the words are selected on the basis of their spelling patterns.

Words that have irregular spellings are thought of as sight words.

Teachers are encouraged to have the children do much writing, using word patterns they have read.

Work in syntax is also stressed. This would be done by having the children read sentences where the word order is changed.

> Man is by the pan.
> Is Nan by the pan?
> The pan is by Nan.

In essence most linguistic programs for reading begin with language activities. The alphabet letters, both capital and lower-case forms, are learned. Words are introduced in spelling patterns. Sentences are then formed, using words previously learned in the patterns.

ADVANTAGES OF THE LINGUISTIC APPROACH

1. The linguistic approach helps a child recognize that reading is talk written down. The linguistic approach is concerned with the relationship between phonemes and graphemes.

2. A linguistic approach begins with familiar words that are phonemically regular then progresses through semi-regular and irregular spellings.

3. This emphasis on using regular spelling patterns as much as possible in the early stages of reading permits the child to respond to visual patterns automatically and thus read more for comprehension.

4. The approach stresses that words should be read as wholes and when a new word is presented it is first spelled by saying the letters and not sounding the letters out. Thus the child experiences less confusion.

5. The child learns that the way letters function is controlled by the arrangement of these letters in a word.

6. The linguistic approach develops an awareness in the child of sentence order—subjects, verbs, and complements.

7. It helps children break "the code" by discovering written language is merely spoken language set down in written code.

8. Linguists feel this is a "natural" way to teach reading, for children have a built-in knowledge of their own language.

DISADVANTAGES OF THE LINGUISTIC APPROACH

1. One of the greatest disadvantages is that we cannot label a linguistic approach. Not all linguists agree with each other on one methodology of teaching reading.

2. Theories relative to instructional materials and methodology have not been extensively field-tested in classrooms.

3. The vocabulary is so carefully controlled that it does not take into account the working vocabularies of the children.

4. Primary children's eyes fixate two times per word, not letter-by-letter as some linguists advocate.

5. Word-by-word reading is encouraged.

6. The use of nonsense words and phrases deemphasizes reading for comprehension. Research has shown it is easier to learn and retain meaningful words than nonsense words.

7. Little emphasis is placed on reading for meaning at the beginning stages of reading. Linguists feel reading is a process of decoding, thus this is the major emphasis.

8. Success in reading is not completely dependent upon auditory memory for speech, as the linguistic approach emphasizes.

RESEARCH

Few studies are available that test the effectiveness of a linguistic approach against a control situation.

Chall (3) reports from her review of this limited research:

I would hypothesize from the evidence that their approaches, line systematic phonics, probably give better results than approaches based on introducing sight words first and teaching moderate amounts of phonics in a varied environment of irregularly spelled words. However, to conclude from this that the Bloomfield or Fries programs will prove better than systematic phonics seems questionable. I believe these approaches are effective because they put greater stress on decoding of regularly spelled words as the initial step in learning to read.

SUMMARY

This approach to reading instruction has appeared most recently on the scene. Some linguists, students of spoken language, have extended their study to written language and the "decoding" process of reading this language.

The methods employed in this approach center upon beginning stages of reading. Learning spelling patterns with words and nonsense words is one of the foundations on which the reading instruction is built.

Whether this approach will be expanded and used more completely will probably depend on its development. Materials, organizational plans, in-service programs, skill-training techniques, record-keeping, and evaluation procedures need to be developed. Then, after complete field-testing valid judgments can be made as to its effectiveness.

The approach has brought with it an interest and exploration in linguistics on the part of teachers as to how they might develop proficiency in communication skills within the classroom. This, in itself, has been most advantageous.

REFERENCES

1. Bloomfield, Leonard. "Linguistics and Reading", *Elementary English Review*, XIX (1942). Pp. 125-30, 183-86.
2. Bloomfield, Leonard, and Clarence R. Barnhart. *Let's Read—A Linguistic Approach*. Detroit: Wayne State University Press, 1961.
3. Chall, Jeanne. *Learning to Read: The Great Debate*. New York: McGraw-Hill, 1967. Pp. 115-19.

4. Duffy, Gerald G. *Teaching Linguistics*. Dansville, New York: Instructor Publications, 1969.
5. Harris, Albert J. *How to Increase Reading Ability*. New York: David McKay Company, Inc., 1970. Pp. 70-71.

SUPPLEMENTARY REFERENCES

1. Fries, Charles C. *Linguistics and Reading*. New York: Holt, Rinehart and Winston, 1963.
2. Heilman, Arthur. *Principles and Practices of Teaching Reading*. Columbus, Ohio: Charles E. Merrill Publishing Co. Pp. 235-56.
3. Lefevre, Carl A. *Linguistics and the Teaching of Reading*. New York: McGraw-Hill, 1964.
4. Sabaroff, Rose E. "Improving Achievement in Beginning Reading: A Linguistic Approach," *The Reading Teacher*, XXIII (March, 1970). Pp. 523-27.
5. Seymour, Dorothy. "The Difference Between Linguistics and Phonics," *The Reading Teacher*, XXIII (November, 1969). Pp. 149-67.

CHAPTER 5

The Phonic Approach

This reading approach has been the center of controversy for over a hundred years. Much has been written concerning this area of reading instruction. The problem in much of this literature is that phonics is not put in its proper perspective. It has either been condemned as a destructive method leading to slow, word-by-word readers who gain little comprehension from the printed page or a panacea for all the reading problems a child may encounter. It is neither. For there is no one phonic method or approach. The content of these approaches differs from author to author. These differences are often the center of the controversy which either sheds criticism or accolades on the entire approach.

DEFINITION

The phonic approach is one section of the whole beginning reading act. It is a method for teaching word recognition. The goal is to give the child a key to independently unlock unfamiliar words so that meaning and reading pleasure will come to him.

The phonic approach teaches word recognition as a sounding-blending process. Under this method of instruction, the child is usually given ear training to make sure that he attends to and learns that words are made up of individual sounds. He then is taught beginning sounds of words, vowel and consonant sounds, and phonic blends. In some of the most strict applications of this method, this instruction is limited to drill on these elements. The child has some familiarity with these sounds, the sounds are combined and blended into words, the child sounds out the words. The words are then combined into sentences. When reading sentences the child

44

should use the sounding procedure only when attacking an unfamiliar word. The child continues to develop this system of word recognition which eventually makes him an independent reader.

THE ROLE OF THE TEACHER

The teacher's role in the phonic approach, as in any other approach, is that she holds the key to success. Research (5) has shown some disturbing evidence that many teachers are not adequately trained in the phonics skills they are teaching. Thus, much of their classroom success is dependent on their own study of the materials and manuals provided.

It might be advantageous to briefly define and list the phonic elements commonly used in this approach:

boy	Single consonants – In a simple definition, all those
dog	alphabetic letters that are not vowels.
black	Consonant blends – Two or three consonants whose
street	sounds are blended.
phone	Consonant digraphs – A combination of consonant let-
bring	ters which produce a single sound unlike the sound
	associated with either of the two letters.
	Vowels – The vowels are a, e, i, o, u. Generally, every
	syllable contains a sounded vowel.
auto	Vowel digraphs – A vowel combination which has a
moon	different sound from either vowel but requires no
	change in mouth position.
boy	Dipthongs – Two vowels recording a sound unlike
oil	that of either vowel, that sound requiring a change in
	the mouth position.

In the actual methodology employed in the phonic approach, the teacher uses either the synthetic method or the analytic method.

The Synthetic Method – This method is most often associated with the phonic approach. Children are taught the sounds of letters and how to combine or synthesize them into words. The process begins with individual letters and progresses to words.

The Analytic Method—Sometimes this method has had sub-groups—the word method, the phrase method, and the sentence method. In relation to its usage with the phonic approach, it begins with words that the children know, and from these words generalizations are drawn on the basis of similar phonic elements. Then new words are introduced using these elements. This technique attempts to avoid the problems encountered with sounding and blending.

ADVANTAGES OF THE PHONIC APPROACH

1. It develops efficiency in word recognition.
2. It develops independence in recognizing new words.
3. Interest continues in reading, as the child can unlock new words without frustration.
4. Child sees the association between printed letters and the speech sounds they represent.

DISADVANTAGES OF THE PHONIC APPROACH

1. Phonics tend to isolate speech sounds in a completely unnatural, unspeechlike manner. Blending the sounds is often more confusing than helpful.
2. Very often there is too much repetition of phonic elements. It can become very boring and tedious for the children if there is no variation.
3. Children learn to read word-by-word. Worrying about pronunciation more than reading for comprehension is often a habit hard to break.
4. With many exceptions to the rules, children can easily be confused.

RESEARCH

Before reviewing briefly some major statements made concerning research on this approach, we must take into consideration the vast differences in implementation of phonic instruction.

Phonic methods have in common a stress on word recognition through the learning of the phonemic equivalents of letters and letter groups and the application of phonic rules. They differ among themselves on many important issues, such as whether to begin with consonants or vowels, whether to teach short vowels before long vowels or vice versa; how many rules to teach; which rules, and in which order; whether to use a whole-word phonics procedure or a synthetic sounding-blending procedure; when to introduce meaningful material; and so on. While the placing of emphasis on phonics may be described as an approach to the teaching of beginning reading, there is little agreement among phonic methods on details. (5, p. 70)

Dr. Jeanne Chall (1) in her massive research review in the area of reading makes an interesting statement in regard to her findings and the importance of phonic instruction.

My review of the research from the laboratory, the classroom, and the clinic points to the need for a correction in beginning reading instructional methods. Most school children in the United States are taught to read by what I have termed a meaning-emphasis method. Yet the research from 1912 to 1965 indicates that a code-emphasis method — i.e., one that views beginning reading as essentially different from mature reading and emphasizes learning of the printed code for the spoken language — produces better results at least up to the point where sufficient evidence seems to be available, the end of the third grade. Nor can I emphasize too strongly that I recommend a code emphasis only as a beginning reading method — a method to start the child on — and I do not recommend ignoring reading-for-meaning practice.

Gates and Russell (4) showed in their research that there can be too much emphasis on phonics even in a combined program. The study found that pupils who were taught the phonetic method were superior in their attention to small details of words but inferior in comprehension. This should show us that phonics should never be employed as a sole method at any level.

SUMMARY

Edward Dolch (3), Professor of Education at the University of Illinois states:

> To be a good reader, a child must be able to sound out new words. A child may increase his vocabulary by sight methods, but sooner or later, he will have to attack new words by himself. Beginning sounding after a certain number of sight words are known, means we must first teach the habit of seeing words as wholes, and then keep that habit in spite of sounding parts. Phonics readiness comes later than readiness for sight learning, and is reached at about seven years mental age.

Although the phonic approach is as varied as the teacher and materials used, we see from research and reading experts the agreement that it is an important part of the beginning reading program. Its ability to help children attack new words independently is a prime objective.

DeBoer (2) lists some principles for teaching phonics which summarize this approach very well.

> Principles of teaching phonics — generalizations
> 1. Instruction in phonics should be functional.
> 2. For most pupils, instruction in phonics should be systematic. This progression should be from the simpler, more widely used elements and generalizations to the more difficult and less generally applied learnings, with well-distributed practice.
> 3. The work in phonics should be adapted to individual differences.
> 4. Rules and generalizations should frequently be taught inductively.

REFERENCES

1. Chall, Jeanne. *Learning to Read: The Great Debate.* New York: McGraw-Hill, 1967. P. 307.

2. De Boer, John J., and Martha Dallmann. *The Teaching of Reading*. New York: Holt, Rinehart and Winston, Inc., 1970. Pp. 123-24.
3. Dolch, E. W. *Psychology and the Teaching of Reading*, second edition. Champaign, Ill.: The Garrard Press, 1951.
4. Gates, A. I., and Russell, D. H. "Types of Material, Vocabulary Burden, Word Analysis and Other Factors in Beginning Reading," *Elementary School Journal*, 1938. Vol. 39, pp. 119-28.
5. Harris, Albert J. *How to Increase Reading Ability*. New York: David McKay Company, 1970.

SUPPLEMENTARY REFERENCES

1. Clyner, Theodore. "The Utility of Phonic Generalizations in the Primary Grades," *The Reading Teacher*, 16, January, 1963. Pp. 252-58.
2. Gans, Roma. *Fact and Fiction About Phonics*. Indianapolis, Indiana: The Bobbs-Merrill Company, Inc., 1964.
3. Hildreth, Gertrude "New Methods for Old in Teaching Phonics," *Elementary School Journal*, 57, May, 1957. Pp. 436-41.
4. Stauffer, Russell G. *Directing Reading Maturity as a Cognitive Process*. New York: Harper & Row, Publishers, Inc., 1969. Chapter 6.
5. Tinker, Miles A., and Constance M. McCullough. *Teaching Elementary Reading*. New York: Appleton-Century-Crofts, 1968. Pp. 130-84.

CHAPTER 6

The Alphabetic Approach

No matter what approach is used in teaching reading, teachers quickly realize problems are increased because of the lack of consistent correspondence between the spelling and pronunciation of American English. Each letter in our language does not always have just one sound.

This concern and need for reform of our language has been present for many years. Lately, we have seen some dramatic ideas materialize in reading. We will briefly define some of these innovative programs, but center our discussion on the most widely used—the Initial Teaching Alphabet.

ALPHABETIC PROGRAMS

1. UNIFON—(6) This is a 40-letter alphabet, each letter producing a sound. Capital letters are used exclusively. Long vowels, diphthongs, and th, ch, sh, and ng sounds have new symbols. All silent and double letters are dropped; short vowels are represented by regular symbols.

2. Diacritical Marking System—(3) This beginning reading system adds diacritical marks to the letters in the traditional alphabet. The basic rules are:

    a. Regular consonants and short vowels are unchanged.
    b. Silent letters have a slash mark.
    c. Long vowels have a bar over mark.
    d. Schwa vowels have a dot over mark.
    e. Other consistent sounds than those above are indicated by the bar.

f. Digraphs have a bar under both letters.

g. Exceptions to the above stated basic rules have an asterisk above the letter.

An example of this system is given below:

THĖ LITTLₑ RED HEN

⁎̲Ȯnce upon a tīmₑ Littlₑ Red Hen livₑd in a ba̲r̲n wit̲h̲ hₑr fivₑ chiₑks.

3. Ten-Vowel Alphabet—(1) Using letters for short vowels and capitals for long vowels, the author is trying to simplify phonetic problems. He also drops all silent and doubled letters, uses k for a hard c sound, z for hard s sound and f for the ph sound. The author has published his own materials through Carlton Press.

4. Laubach's Alphabet—(5) In this system, Laubach inserts a slant line after each long vowel, spells other vowel combinations phonetically and omits silent letters. An example would be:

Yoo might suppo/z that the/ ordina/ry ty/pri/ter wuud not hav e/nuff letterz for every wun ov the/ Ingglish soundz.

5. Words in Color—(4) This approach is really a combination of an alphabet-phonic system. From the company literature it is described below:

Each of the forty-seven sounds of English is printed in a distinctive color on wall charts. Alphabet letters or groups of letters are colored according to how they sound in a given word. Thus color is used to make English phonetic without in any way changing traditional spellings.

A sound is always represented by one color—regardless of its spelling. If it is the short sound of "a", it is white whether it is in "pat" or "laugh." Children use these color clues to help them fix the image in their minds.

From the beginning, the pupil writes and reads in black and white each colored sign that he is introduced to so that there is immediate and constant transfer. Since he carries the images of these signs in color in his mind, the pupil can evoke and re-evoke the images if he needs them for reading or writing. Thus he is not dependent on printing in color.

6. The Initial Teaching Alphabet—Ten years ago, Sir James Pitman introduced the Initial Teaching Alphabet (ITA) as a device to aid in the teaching of reading in England. It was introduced into the United States' school system two years later by John Downing and has since been used in many schools. It should be noted, however, that there are differences in the English and American systems.

ITA is not a method of reading instruction, but rather a tool to be used by the teacher in any method he chooses. It is merely what the name implies, an alphabet. It is designed to simplify beginning reading by eliminating the discrepancies between the 40-odd sounds in the English language and the more than 2,000 varied spellings that represent those sounds. A one-to-one relationship between letters seen and speech sounds heard is the result. There is only one letter character for each sound.

ITA uses 44 symbols instead of the traditional 26. Of these 44 symbols 24 are traditional, 14 look like traditional letters joined together, and the remaining "new" symbols represent special English phonemes such as the "th" sound and the "ch" sound. Capital letters are eliminated and a larger version of the letter becomes the "capital." The letters "x" and "q" are eliminated.

Some examples of words in ITA:

was	woz
large	larj
laugh	laf
one	wun

THE ROLE OF THE TEACHER

In addition to the task of learning the alphabet herself, the teacher's main role is implementing its use into the reading program. This alphabet, as previously stated, is used only for beginning reading.

The teacher must know each child's proficiency so that as soon as he is reading well enough in ITA a transition is begun to traditional materials. The teacher's professional judgment is the criterion for the transition.

Provision for creative expression using ITA should definitely be a part of the teacher's role. This self-expression part of the program has met with much success.

ADVANTAGES OF ITA

1. It is simpler for a child to learn to read when every symbol being read is represented by one sound.

2. Children develop greater skill in creative self-expression.

3. Increases enthusiasm for reading and interest in books because the child finds success.

4. The alphabet can be used with other methods or approaches.

5. Children learn to read more rapidly with ITA than with the traditional alphabet.

DISADVANTAGES OF ITA

1. It is not a method, but the techniques and materials should be more clearly defined as to their use with other systems.

2. The transition from ITA to the traditional alphabet is not as easy as the literature might indicate.

3. It is expensive because it means buying new reading books written in the ITA alphabet and also library books.

4. Outside the school, children will see the traditional alphabet. This could be confusing.

5. It has not been used long enough in the United States to justify its superiority as claimed.

RESEARCH

One of the biggest criticisms with studies made using ITA (2) is the lack of control in the variables in experimental and control groups.

Spache (7) states in reviewing the research:

Five of the first grade reading studies sponsored by the Office of Education employed ITA materials in their contrasts of methods. Only one used the British-designed materials; all others, the American version. In the one study using the British system, all differences favored the ITA approach. In the other studies, performances were significantly different only in word recognition and at equal levels in comprehension, spelling, and rate and accuracy of oral reading. Unlike the other four, the study utilizing the British system produced significant superiority in spelling in traditional orthography. In four of the five studies, tests of knowledge of phonics skills favored ITA.

SUMMARY

This area of reading instruction has greatly increased during the last few years. Until research validly shows their importance we must keep the following points in mind:

1. Most alphabetic approaches are not methods but a "decoding" system.
2. These approaches can be used with any method.
3. Often children have developed proficient creative writing skills due to the alphabet employed.

We should be aware of their use and evaluate on the basis of future research and development.

REFERENCES

1. Davis, Leo G. *New England Orthografy*. New York: Carlton Press.
2. De Boer, John J., and Martha Dallmann. *The Teaching of Reading*. New York: Holt, Rinehart and Winston, 1970. P. 109.
3. Fry, Edward. "A Diacritical Marking System to Aid Beginning Reading Instruction," *Elementary English*, 41 (May, 1964). Pp. 526-29.
4. Gattegno, Calet. *Words in Color*. Chicago: Learning Materials, Inc., 1962.
5. Laubach, Frank C. "Progress Toward World-Wide Literacy" in *New Developments in Programs and Procedures for College — Adult Reading*. Pp. 87-99. Twelfth Yearbook of the National

Reading Conference, 1963.

6. Malone, John R. "The Unifon System." *Wilson Library Bulletin,* 40 (September, 1965). Pp. 63-65.

7. Spache, George D., and Evelyn Spache. *Reading in the Elementary School.* Boston: Allyn and Bacon, 1969. Pp. 496-97.

8. Downing, John. *The Initial Teaching Alphabet Reading Experiment.* Chicago: Scott, Foresman and Co., 1964.

SUPPLEMENTARY REFERENCES

1. Downing, John. "How I.T.A. Began," *Elementary English,* 44 (January, 1967). Pp. 40-46.

2. Fry, Edward B. "First Grade Reading Instruction Using Diacritical Marking System, Initial Teaching Alphabet and Basal Reading System," *The Reading Teacher,* 19 (May, 1966). Pp. 666-69.

3. Smith, Nila Banton. "Approaches Differ," *Reading Instruction for Today's Children.* Englewood Cliffs, N.J.: Prentice Hall, 1963. Pp. 79-81.

4. Stewart, Rebecca W. "I.T.A. — After Two Years," *Elementary English,* 42 (October, 1965). Pp. 660-65.

CHAPTER 7

The Programmed Instruction Approach

This approach to the teaching of reading was introduced in the 1950s. It has not shown any tremendous effect on classroom teaching as yet. Reasons for this could be that the programmed materials are often used in connection with another method or approach. Also, used as a separate reading approach, research has not been able to show that it produces better readers than other methods. The possibilities of using these self-instructional, self-correcting materials need to be further explored and researched.

DEFINITION

Programmed reading materials can be in a workbook-type format or processed for a machine. Very often the expense of a teaching machine prohibits its use. These may be a simple mechanical device or a very elaborate electronic machine that has the programmed material on microfilm and audio-tape.

In the case of reading instruction most materials are in workbook form. These have the advantage of being usable in the library, in the classroom, or at home. The child also has accessibility to the materials when he needs them, rather than waiting for an available machine.

The subject matter of the material is presented in very small, sequential (programmed) steps. Each step is a small unit called a frame. Each frame requires some type of response from the child. This may be supplying a missing word in a sentence, answering a question, responding to a true-false or multiple choice question. Programmed materials for machines are answered by pushing a button, pulling a lever, or some other operation.

After responding to the answer required in the frame, the child gets immediate feedback on his success or failure. This is done by various ways, as uncovering an answer mask or checking marginal answers. Each successive step in the material is dependent upon the mastery of the previous one. Thus, the immediate feedback is an essential reinforcement ingredient of programmed materials. There is much repetition and review and emphasis falls on having the child succeed and continue at his own pace.

In reading, available programmed materials are limited. One example (1) is characterized by both a linguistic and phonic emphasis. The reading vocabulary in the material is selected by spelling patterns (Nan, pan, tan, etc.). Sounds of individual letters are also emphasized. The reading of individual sentences is used for practice in the programmed frames. Stories are not used in the beginning programmed materials.

Other programmed materials available deal with basic reading skills of word recognition, phonetic analysis, context clues, and structural analysis.

THE ROLE OF THE TEACHER

"Self-teaching" is a term used to describe programmed materials. If this is truly the case, what is the role of the teacher?

The first step is directing the use of the materials themselves. There are programmed materials for beginning reading skills through upper-level skills. In beginning stages of learning, the children need a great deal of teacher guidance before they would be able to independently work through the materials.

The potential offered the classroom teacher by using programmed materials is great in that she is now free to spend her time in one-to-one or small-group instruction, depending on the need. Thus, the teacher is freed from repetitive drill situations and can work on more important aspects of instruction.

The whole role of the teacher changes when the individualized, programmed approach is used. Her role becomes one of a counselor, guide, diagnostician, motivator, and prescriber. Providing each child with materials appropriate for him is a key to the success of the approach.

ADVANTAGES OF THE PROGRAMMED
INSTRUCTION APPROACH

1. Each child proceeds at his own pace.

2. Reinforcement (positive or correction) would be given to every child at each step of learning.

3. A child's errors would be recorded, giving the teacher a picture of where the student was having trouble.

4. Completed programs can be used as a record of progress.

5. Self-instructional, in that its contents need not be explained, reviewed, or repeated by other instructional materials or teachers.

6. Permits the teacher to help individual pupils or small groups because all the children are working in their own workbooks.

7. Teachers will understand the components and sequence of reading skills with greater clarity by using the materials.

DISADVANTAGES OF THE PROGRAMMED
INSTRUCTION APPROACH

1. The controlled research on its use is very scant.

2. Some children do not have the attention span to work at these materials for the designated period.

3. The beginning high motivation level is short-lived.

4. Reading the short, independent frames detracts from the growth of reading phrases or long passages, or skimming for specific facts.

5. Mature comprehension skills in reading would be most difficult to program. Critical analysis and interpretation need the verbal interaction discussion provides.

6. It is doubtful that programming is suitable for developing tastes and interests in reading.

RESEARCH

Research is very limited in regard to controlled situations using programmed reading materials. The lack of field tests hampers evaluation even more.

Dr. Edward Fry (3) reported in his research survey that a developmental reading program yielded results as good but no better than a balanced reading program. The teacher may use programmed reading materials but should not expect greater gains than good teaching can produce without the programmed approach.

Ruddell (2) studied progress comparing three groups of children using the Sullivan *Programmed Reading Series,* a basal series, or a linguistic approach. In this study, sponsored by the U.S. Office of Education, the researcher found mixed results when the reading achievement of first-grade children using programmed materials was compared with the achievement of those using basal materials. The results showed the difference was not significant.

In reviewing the few studies completed, it is important to remember the difficulty to determine what element produces growth. In regard to programmed materials, it might be the programming, the format, the content, or combinations that produced the results.

SUMMARY

The programmed reading approach is relatively new and, as has been mentioned, the research is limited as to its effectiveness. With the continued stress in education on individualization and meeting the needs of each child, this is certainly one approach that should be considered. Teachers should familiarize themselves with these materials. From their critique we may find the most effective way of using this approach with boys and girls.

REFERENCES

1. Buchanan, Cynthia Dee, and Sullivan Associates. *Programmed Reading.* Webster Division, McGraw-Hill.
2. Ruddell, Robert B. *The Effect of Four Programs of Reading Instruction with Varying Emphasis on the Regularity of Grapheme-Phoneme Correspondences and the Relation of the Language Structure to the Meaning on Adjustment on First Grade Reading,* Report of Research Project No. 2699. Berkeley, California, 1965.

3. Tinker, Miles A., and Constance M. McCullough. *Teaching Elementary Reading,* third edition. New York: Appleton-Century-Crofts, 1968. Pp. 332-33.

SUPPLEMENTARY REFERENCES

1. Buchanan, Cynthia Dee. "Programmed Reading," *A Decade of Innovations,* Newark, Del.: International Reading Association, 1968. Pp. 227-33.
2. Hardy, Robert. "Programmed Instruction and Independent Study," *Illinois Journal of Education* (Feb. 1970). Pp. 5-7.
3. Sullivan Associates, "Programmed Learning in Reading," *Programmed Instruction.* Allen D. Calvin, ed. Bloomington, Indiana: University Press, 1969. Pp. 101-37.

CHAPTER 8

Preschool Reading Approaches

When should a child learn to read? This question has been the center of discussion for many years and continues to be unsettled. Many people are now questioning whether the home should begin some reading instruction with pre-kindergarten children. For many children, these preschool years mark the start of their ability to read. In this section we will explore some of the most controversial preschool approaches and some related research.

DEFINITION

Part of the problem in answering the question of when should reading instruction begin lies in the definition of reading. For many years we have separated reading skills from "readiness" skills, the latter in reference to the period of getting ready to read. There are so many skills that intertwine between "getting ready to read" and "reading" that a clear definition of which skill is reading and which is not is most difficult. Some teachers consider learning the alphabet and the sounds represented by each letter as part of reading readiness. Other educators sincerely believe this is a reading process. Thus, when educators and laymen discuss preschool reading, it is often misinterpreted because their terminology for "reading" is not clearly defined.

ROLE OF THE TEACHER

Dependent on the approach used, the teacher may be a professional teacher, a parent, or an instructional aide. The role of the instructor will be defined within the exploration of some of the preschool reading approaches.

One of the most controversial approaches to preschool reading is one that can be purchased in kit form from a national mail-order catalog or woman's magazine coupon. This approach first appeared in the *Ladies Home Journal,* entitled "You Can Teach Your Baby to Read" (1). The authors later expanded their philosophy and methods into the book *How to Teach Your Child to Read* (2). Their position on when to teach a child reading illustrates their philosophy.

> The best time to teach your child to read with little or no trouble is when he is about two years old. Beyond two years of age, the teaching of reading gets harder every year. If your child is five, it will be easier than when he is six. Four is easier still, and three is even easier. If you are willing to go to a little trouble, you can begin when your baby is eighteen months old or, if you are very clever, as early as ten months.

Essentially the method employed is having the child recognize letters or words as they represent his body parts or objects close to him. The child learns "toes" by responding to the printed word and pointing to his toes. Actual objects are used as the child recognizes words on sight. Mother, most often, is the teacher working with the child many times a day.

Another preschool reading approach was done in Denver (8). Through the use of television classes, parents were taught teaching procedures to use with their preschool children in recognizing letters and their sounds and how to identify words. The child watched a weekly 30-minute lesson for 16 weeks. The parents supplemented with activities prepared in a guidebook. The results proved to be quite successful as used with four-year-olds.

Dr. O. K. Moore, a Rutgers sociologist, was researching how humans could learn through a responsive environment. His study centered on his belief that (5) "children between the ages of two and six have a tremendous untapped capacity for learning, and, if placed in a responsive environment can make amazing progress."

Dr. Moore proceeded to test his theory by using a talking typewriter with three- and four-year-old children. The children were teaching themselves how to read with this typewriter. The children worked at individual study booths with typewriter keyboards. The machine was programmed for both an oral and written response. For example: when the letter D appears and is spoken by the machine, the child can press only the D key. None of the other keys will work. In spelling a word, as dog, he can depress only the letters d-o-g and in that order. Eventually the child writes sentences and paragraphs, which he can read.

The typewriter in itself is under experimentation by several school districts at present. It looks like a regular typewriter with a large keyboard. There is a screen and microphone attached to the typewriter and controlled by a computer. The cost is $40,000, but it can be leased.

Young children would be very motivated with this approach. They are active and self-directed and experience success in correct responses. Dr. Moore claims much success with this approach.

ADVANTAGES OF PRESCHOOL READING

1. A child who has a good command of his oral language ought to be able to read. Proponents feel very strongly that if language is fairly well established in three or four years, reading could be started at this time.

2. If a child's desire to read is pronounced he will learn to read without being enrolled in school. There is doubt he will be harmed by not having professional training.

3. The younger the child the easier it is to teach him to read. This is one of the claims made by Doman, as previously mentioned.

4. Preschool readers continue to lead in achievement over those who did not begin reading until first grade. Many facets of this claim can be challenged, for it depends on the caliber of instruction, ability, environment, etc.

DISADVANTAGES OF PRESCHOOL READING

1. Parents are not professionally trained in the teaching of reading. This relates to our introductory statement concerning the

definition of reading. Many "reading" skills can be taught at home, that is, exposure to books, being read to, identification of labels and alphabet letters and the sounds they make.

2. Preschool reading will be harmful to a child's vision. There is a lack of pertinent research in this area to either support or refute this point.

3. Preschool reading leads to boredom in school. This depends on the professional skill of the teacher to see that the child is correctly placed in a group where he will be challenged and his learning needs met.

4. James Hymes (6) expresses his views in stating a word of caution: "Everyone loses if we produce early readers but in the process weaken humans. Everyone loses if we produce early readers but in the process kill the joy of reading."

RESEARCH

The Gallup Studies of Early Childhood (4) were conducted in 1969, interviewing mothers of preschool children to gain support for early reading instruction. It was found that most of the top first-grade pupils had been read to at regular intervals before they entered first grade. Other items found to be significant with those top achievers were parents that read for enjoyment and an abundance of books and magazines. One conclusion from this study indicates that a child as early as the age of one has a head start statistically to be a successful reader if exposed to this type of environment.

There are two major studies in the area of preschool reading that must be included in our survey: The Denver Studies and Durkin's Study.

The Denver Studies (8) done in 1966 evaluated (a) programs of reading instruction to kindergarten children and (b) television programs as a preschool reading program with parental guidance. In both instances the sample children were achieving more in first grade than those who had had no preschool or kindergarten training.

Dolores Durkin (3) studied children who had learned to read before going to school. She found many of these children had average intelligence but were inquisitive. Their questions about names of things, words in books, labels were answered by parents or older brothers and sisters.

Some of the children in the study learned to read with only casual or incidental help, others had more formal training. The exposure to reading materials apparently held their interest in books and reading, for Durkin found that generally these preschool readers did achieve more in reading than those who had not been preschool readers.

SUMMARY

Evidence has shown that some children do learn to read earlier than other boys and girls. The discussion still continues as to whether it is desirable for them to read at an early age or not. But those children who are ready to read will develop many beginning reading skills.

We have seen how "Sesame Street" has developed an awareness in the public of pre-reading skills. Hopefully, this awareness will not develop into parental pressure on the child to read. More than parental pride in the child's achievement must be the reason for preschool reading.

Parents are genuinely concerned in wanting to provide experiences for their child so that reading will be a successful, enjoyable experience.

McCullough (9) gives some suggestions to parents:

> Experience and guidance prior to kindergarten can influence greatly the development of reading readiness. The degree to which readiness develops during the first five or six years depends upon the child-parent relationship, kind of home and neighborhood.

The home environmental effects upon reading readiness during the preschool years and after may be such that they foster the development of excellent reading readiness, only partial readiness, or hardly any at all, depending upon the nature of the home and what goes on in it. Several ways in which readiness is likely to develop from some activities include the following:

1. Growth of vocabulary and concept development. The child begins early to learn the meaning of words and the concepts they embody. He hears words spoken in relation to objects and to his activities and experiences. Guidance is given by parents and others who answer questions, correct mistakes, and give encouragement.

2. Verbal facility tends to develop hand-in-hand with growth in vocabulary and concepts. A child learns to talk by talking. Parents should encourage children to put their experiences into words and steer them into the sorts of activities that foster talking. In all this, clear enunciation is important, that is, baby talk should be discouraged.

3. Learning to listen. Numerous activities, such as conversing with parents and others, telling or reading stories to him, and giving directions on how to run an errand, encourage the child to listen.

4. Auditory discrimination. Many opportunities, such as listening to nursery rhymes and to stories told or read by an older person, help a child to recognize similarities and differences between words and sounds.

5. Visual discrimination begins early and improves through the preschool years. The progress is from noting the cruder similarities and differences to the finer discriminations first in objects and pictures, and finally in symbols and words. Eventually, the child learns that a printed word stands for a spoken word.

6. Motor coordination between eyes and hands is developed through such activities as handling toys, scribbling with crayons, and turning pages of books and magazines.

7. Personal and social adjustment develop hand-in-hand. Personal adjustment depends largely upon a feeling of security, a feeling of being loved, inside and outside the home. Social adjustment is derived from participating in a variety of social activities with other children, as in play, parties, Sunday school, etc. Association with adults in the home will develop ease in talking with them.

8. Growth of independence. Overprotection by parents allows the child little chance to learn to do things by himself. This can become a serious handicap on entering school. The child is then far from ready to learn to read, for he is still pretty much a baby. Obviously, parents should foster the development of independence in their children.

REFERENCES

1. Doman, Glenn, George L. Stevens, and Reginald C. Orem. "You Can Teach Your Baby to Read," *Ladies Home Journal*, 80 (May, 1963). P. 62.
2. Doman, Glenn. *How to Teach Your Child to Read*. New York: Random House, Inc., 1964.
3. Durkin, Dolores. "A Study of Children Who Learned to Read Prior to First Grade," *California Journal of Educational Research*, 10 (May, 1959). Pp. 109-13.
4. "Early Childhood Education Issue." IDEA Reporter (Winter, 1969). P. 2.
5. Frost, Joe L. (ed.). *Issues and Innovations in the Teaching of Reading*. Glenview, Illinois: Scott, Foresman and Co., 1967. Pp. 110-16.
6. Hymes, James L., Jr. "Early Reading Is a Very Risky Business," *Grade Teacher*, 82 (March, 1965). P. 88.
7. McKee, P., and J. E. Brzeinski. *The Effectiveness of Teaching Reading in Kindergarten*, Cooperative Research Project No. 5-0371. Denver Public Schools, 1966.
8. McManua, Anastasia. "The Denver Prereading Project Conducted by WENH-TV," *The Reading Teacher*, 18 (October, 1964). Pp. 22-26.
9. Tinker, Miles A., and Constance McCullough. *Teaching Elementary Reading*. New York: Apple-Century-Crofts, 1968. Pp. 90-91.

SUPPLEMENTARY REFERENCES

1. Education Section, "O.K.'s Children," *Time* (November 7, 1960). P. 103.
2. Gates, Arthur I. "Unsolved Problems in Reading: A Symposium," *Elementary English* (October, 1954). Pp. 331-34.
3. Hurd, G. M., and Rimmel, E. L. *Preparing Your Child for Reading*. Denver: Denver Public Schools, 1961.
4. Terman, Sibyl, and Walcutt, C. C. *Reading: Chaos and Cure*. New York: McGraw-Hill Book Co., Inc. 1958.

CHAPTER 9

Reading Approaches for the
Disadvantaged

The 1960s brought a revived interest in an old educational problem: children from lower socioeconomic areas start school with decidedly proven academic disadvantages. The outcome of this renewed interest was formalized in the government-supported projects of Head Start and Follow Through. Because we have taken a closer look at these children, we have also looked at our methods and materials, realizing adaptation to the needs of these children was necessary.

DEFINITION

Much is now being written about the "disadvantaged reader" or the "disadvantaged child." We find there are many and various kinds of "disadvantaged" learners. Usually, these children are identified by scoring very low on achievement tests. They are disadvantaged as learners. The disadvantage may be caused from physical or emotional problems, economic or family problems. Some children may be disadvantaged because of language. Many programs and materials are now being tried in schools across the country aiming at raising low achievers' performance levels.

THE ROLE OF THE TEACHER

As has been stated previously, the key factor in any approach is the teacher. Working with disadvantaged children, the teacher still holds the key. Building in successful experiences for each child within an environment of sincere care for the worth of that child is the teacher's focal point.

Goldberg (1) has listed approaches she considers to be successful for the teacher to use with disadvantaged children:

1. Each pupil's status in each learning area has to be ascertained. Teaching must begin where the pupil is, regardless of grade level-age differential, and materials must be appropriate to his knowledge derived from home or neighborhood experiences.

2. Each pupil merits respect as a person, appreciation of his efforts, and understanding of his problems. The teacher must not show by word, look, or gesture that the child's inability to perform adequately or his lack of comprehension of even the most rudimentary concepts is shocking or disturbing.

3. All procedures need to be paced in accordance with the pupil's speed of learning. No assumptions should be made that the child has grasped what has been taught until he is able to demonstrate his grasp over and over again in a variety of contexts.

4. The learning situation needs to have a high degree of structure and consistency so that the child knows what is expected of him at all times and is neither confused nor tempted to test the limits through inappropriate behavior.

5. The learning situation should provide a maximum of positive reinforcement and a minimum of negative reinforcement. Self-teaching materials as well as the teacher should confront the learner with as few tests as possible in which there is a high probability of error.

6. The classroom as well as the after-school learning activities should provide as much one-to-one, teacher-pupil learning contact as possible.

7. Materials should be related to the world of the learner but not limited to his immediate environment. Stories about cowboys and rockets may prove more exciting and thus a better learning medium than those about the local firehouse and the sanitation truck.

8. Although the school should start where the learner is, the responsibility of education in a democracy is to enable him to move as far as he can go, which is often much farther than he himself regards as his limit.

MATERIALS

For years basal reading materials were geared for white, middle-class children living in suburbia. Many non-white urban children had no way of identifying with these characters in their reading books. With the recent emphasis on identification and help for the disadvantaged child, several companies now have developed materials for these children.

Prepared by the Bank Street College of Education, *The Bank Street Readers* are said to provide readers with material that is multi-racial and multi-cultural. This material was published by a company that already had published a more traditional basal reader.

Several publishers have now seen the need to develop some multi-racial materials. Many have not altered content but changed the illustrations to include multi-racial children and adults. We don't have evidence as to how successful these materials have been. Content should also be altered to meet situations and experiences with which these children can identify.

One series that has geared the content to experiences of the urban disadvantaged child is the *City Schools Reading Program*. The feeling that success in reading will come with more familiar content and pictures is the goal of this program.

RESEARCH

Several studies (2) and informal accounts point to the fact that the teacher is the most important factor in the reading program for disadvantaged children. As with all children, the research points out that disadvantaged children learn to read in various different methods.

SUMMARY

With the teacher always as the key to a successful reading experience, it is even more important that the disadvantaged learner have the benefit of excellent teachers. Children respond to teachers who care about them and accept them for themselves. Children need to develop this feeling of success and self-worth in a friendly atmosphere. So often teachers of mediocre ability are placed in "disadvantaged" areas only to become discouraged and leave. This is where we need the real professional who can develop in these children a love for learning that will last a lifetime.

REFERENCES

1. Frazier, Alexander (ed.). *Educating the Children of the Poor.* Washington, D.C.: Association for Supervision and Curriculum Development, 1968. Pp. 15-16.
2. Whipple, Gertrude. "Special Needs of Children Without," *Reading for Children Without — Our Disadvantaged Youth.* Newark, Del.: International Reading Assoc., 1966. Pp. 1-7.

SUPPLEMENTARY REFERENCES

1. "The Disadvantaged Learner," *The Reading Teacher,* 24 (October, 1970).
2. Mergentime, Charlotte. "Tailoring the Reading Program to Needs of Disadvantaged Pupils," *Improvement of Reading Through Classroom Practice.* Newark, Del.: International Reading Association, 1964.
3. Riessman, Frank. *The Culturally Deprived Child.* New York: Harper & Row, 1962.
4. Writers' Committee of the Great Cities School Improvement Program of the Detroit Public Schools. *City Schools Reading Program.* Chicago: Follett Publishing Co., 1964.

Summary

We have briefly given the reader an outline of various reading approaches. Which one is best? Which should be used?

As has been mentioned previously, it is not the approach alone that provides reading success. The key is a teacher who matches the reading approach with the child's needs.

Therefore, the teacher must be familiar with many reading methods and approaches. This task is greatly complicated with all the commercial materials and literature available. Applying method and materials to individual needs takes a very skillful and knowledgeable teacher.

In other words, the successful teacher of reading uses an eclectic approach. No one method is used, but a combination, depending on the needs of the children. We hope that this publication has given the reader some insight into the approaches, emphasizing that no one method has proven far more effective than any other.